Months of the Year

February

by Robyn Brode

Reading consultant: Susan Nations, M.Ed.,
author/literacy coach/consultant

WEEKLY WR READER®
EARLY LEARNING LIBRARY

Please visit our web site at: www.earlyliteracy.cc
For a free color catalog describing Weekly Reader® Early Learning Library's list
of high-quality books, call 1-877-445-5824 (USA) or 1-800-387-3178 (Canada).
Weekly Reader® Early Learning Library's fax: (414) 336-0164.

Library of Congress Cataloging-in-Publication Data

Brode, Robyn.
    February / by Robyn Brode.
      p. cm. — (Months of the year)
    Summary: An introduction to some of the characteristics, events, and activities
of the month of February.
    ISBN 0-8368-3577-8 (lib. bdg.)
    ISBN 0-8368-3613-8 (softcover)
    1. February—Juvenile literature. 2. Holidays—United States—Juvenile literature.
1. February.] I. Title.
GT4803.B765   2003
394.261—dc21   2002034312

First published in 2003 by
Weekly Reader® Early Learning Library
330 West Olive Street, Suite 100
Milwaukee, WI 53212 USA

Editor: Robyn Brode
Art direction, design, and page production: Leonardo Montenegro with Orange Avenue
Models: Olivia Byers-Strans, Isabella Leary, Madeline Leary
Weekly Reader® Early Learning Library art direction: Tammy Gruenewald
Weekly Reader® Early Learning Library editor: Mark J. Sachner

Photo credits: Cover, p. 21 © PictureQuest; title, p. 7 Leonardo Montenegro; p. 9
© Comstock Images; p. 11 © CORBIS; p. 13 (all) © Hulton Archive/Getty Images;
pp. 15, 17, 19 © Getty Images

Printed in the United States of America

1 2 3 4 5 6 7 8 9 07 06 05 04 03

Note to Educators and Parents

Reading is such an exciting adventure for young children! They are beginning to integrate their oral language skills with written language. To help this process along, books must be meaningful, colorful, engaging, and interesting; they should invite young readers to make inquiries about the world around them.

Months of the Year is a new series of books designed to help children learn more about each of the twelve months. In each book, young readers will learn about festivals, celebrations, weather, and other interesting facts about each month.

Each book is specially designed to support the young reader in the reading process. The familiar topics are appealing to young children and invite them to re-read — again and again. The full-color photographs and enhanced text further support the student during the reading process.

These books are designed to be read within an instructional guided reading group. This small group setting allows beginning readers to work with a fluent adult model as they make meaning from the text. After children develop fluency with the text and content, the book can be read independently. Children and adults alike will find these books supportive, engaging, and fun!

— *Susan Nations, M.Ed., author, literacy coach, and consultant in literacy development*

February is the second month of the year. It is also the shortest month. Most of the time, February has only 28 days.

February 2

1	2	3	4	5	6	7
8	9	10	11	12	13	14
15	16	17	18	19	20	21
22	23	24	25	26	27	28

Every four years February has an extra day. This fourth year is called leap year.

February 2

1	2	3	4	5	6	7
8	9	10	11	12	13	14
15	16	17	18	19	20	21
22	23	24	25	26	27	28
29						

February is a winter
month. In some places
it is cold, and it rains
or snows a lot. Where
it is warm, kids play
ball outside.

Every year, February 14 is Valentine's Day. Friends, family, and classmates give each other valentine cards and gifts.

February is Black History Month. It is a time to learn about some famous African Americans.

Do you know about any famous African Americans?

Harriet Tubman   Louis Armstrong   Wilma Rudolph

Presidents' Day is a holiday in February that honors two famous presidents. One of them is Abraham Lincoln. He was born on February 12.

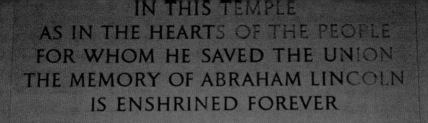

IN THIS TEMPLE
AS IN THE HEARTS OF THE PEOPLE
FOR WHOM HE SAVED THE UNION
THE MEMORY OF ABRAHAM LINCOLN
IS ENSHRINED FOREVER

Statue of Abraham Lincoln

The other president is George Washington. He was born on February 22.

What do you know about these presidents?

Statue of George Washington

In many places,
people attend festivals
in February. They wear
colorful masks
and costumes.

When February ends,
it is time for March
to begin. Soon it will be
time for spring!

Glossary

costumes — clothing that makes a person look like someone else

leap year — a year that occurs every four years, when February has an extra day

Valentine's Day — a day to send cards and gifts to special people

Months of the Year

1	January	7	July
2	**February**	8	August
3	March	9	September
4	April	10	October
5	May	11	November
6	June	12	December

Seasons of the Year

Winter	Summer
Spring	Fall

About the Author

Robyn Brode wrote the *Going Places* children's book series and was the editor for *Get Out!*, which won the 2002 Disney Award for Hands-On Activities. She has been an editor, writer, and teacher in the book publishing field for many years. She earned a Bachelors in English Literature from the University of California at Berkeley.